This book tells the story of

....

Moments to Treasure

MEMORIES & MILESTONES

award

Before I Was Born

My parents thought I would be

....

Names my parents thought of calling me

....

....

....

I came into the world in

..... hours ..... minutes

My hair was

....

My eyes were

....

I've Arrived

My name is

....

....

....

Things in the news on that day

....

Coming Home

.... bought me home

for the first time on ....

at ....

My First Visitors

My First Weeks...

...and Months

Two Hands

 These are my
hand and foot prints
when I was

....

This is me covered
in paint, ready to
do my prints!

 and
Two Feet

The Sweetest Smile

My Naming Day

I was named on

....

by

....

at

....

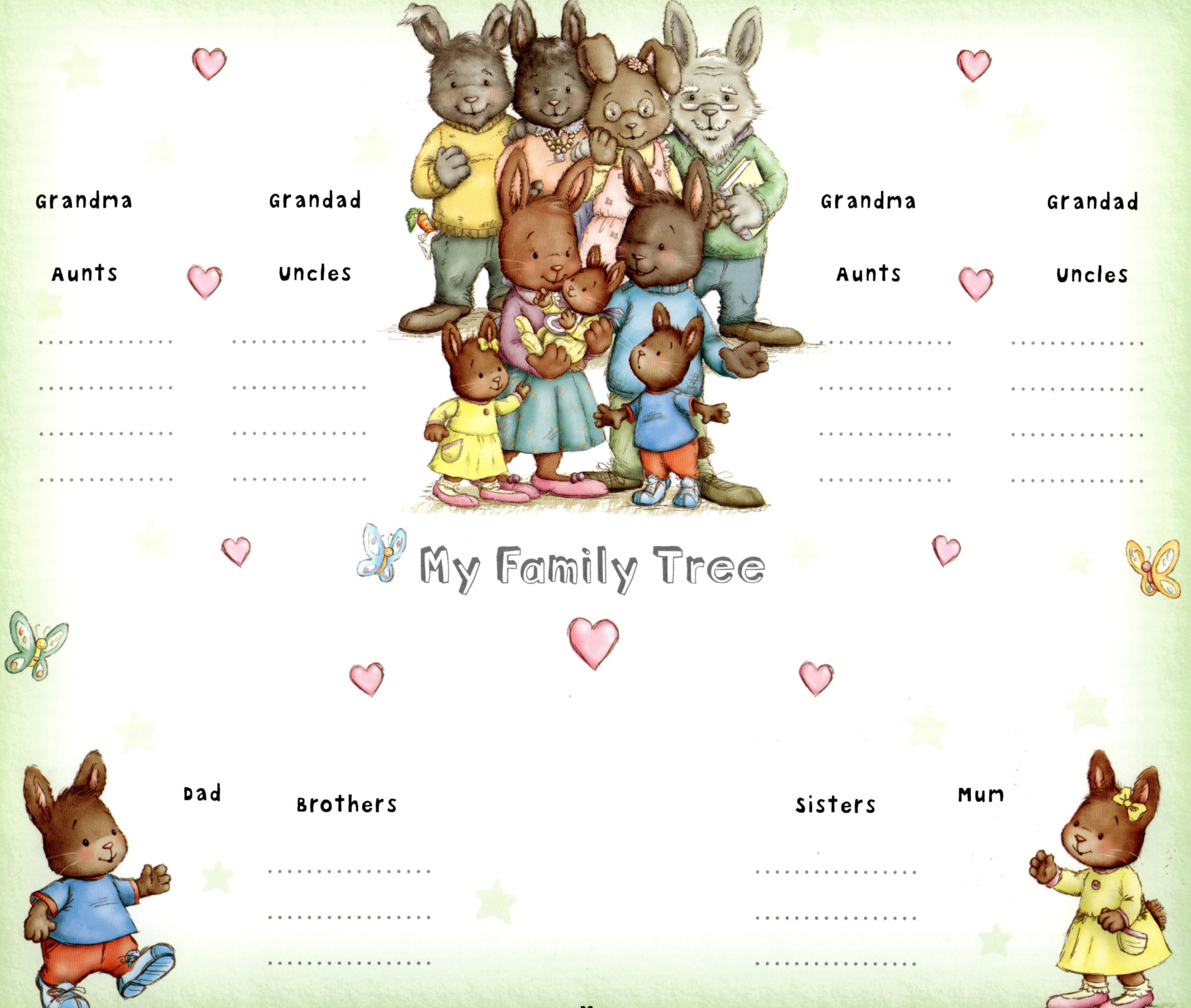

My 'Firsts'

I first crawled on

....

I first stood up on

....

My First Words

I said	It meant
....	....
....	....
....	....

First time I sat up ....

First time I rolled over

....

My first holiday

....

Bath Time

My first time in the big bath

....

My favourite bath toys were

....
....
....

Time to Sleep

Usually I woke up .... times each night

My favourite time to get up was ....

My favourite bedtime toys were

My favourite bedtime song was

My favourite bedtime story was

The first time I slept through the night was

The Things I Did

Health and Growth

Vaccinations I have had   Date

....

....

....

....

I was unwell with

....

....

....

My blood group is ....

My first tooth came through on

....

The things that soothed me
when I was teething were

....

....

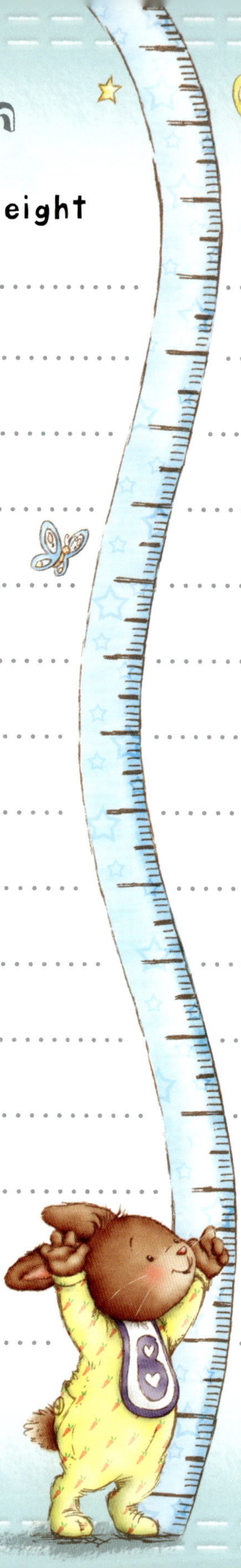

My weight   I measured

.... 1 year

.... 11 months

.... 10 months

.... 9 months

.... 8 months

.... 7 months

.... 6 months

.... 5 months

.... 4 months

.... 3 months

.... 2 months

.... 1 months

.... 2 weeks

.... 1 week

.... birth

Dinner Time!

My first proper food was

....

Yummy Foods   Yukky Foods

....

....

....

Favourite Days

My Very First Birthday

My first party was at

....

The friends who came to my party

....
....
....
....
....
....

I was given lots of lovely gifts!

.... from ....

.... from ....

.... from ....

.... from ....

Illustrated by Angela Hewitt

ISBN 978-1-78270-255-9 My Keepsake Baby Album
ISBN 978-1-78270-256-6 Baby Album and Milestone cards

Copyright © 2019 Award Publications Limited

All rights reserved. No part of this publication may be reproduced or utilised in any form or by any means electronic or mechanical, including photocopying, recording, or by any information storage and retrieval system now known or hereafter invented, without the prior written permission of the publisher.

This edition first published 2019

Published by Award Publications Limited,
The Old Riding School, Welbeck,
Worksop, S80 3LR

www.awardpublications.co.uk

19 1

Printed in china